John's Poetry:
The Heart of an Introvert

John David Hancock

Kingdom Builders Publications LLC

Copyright © 2024 John D. Hancock

Kingdom Builders Publications

All rights reserved. No part of this book may be reproduced or transmitted in any form or by any means without written permission from the author.

ISBN: 979-8-218-38121-9 Soft Copy

LCCN: 2024905015

Printed in the USA

Authored by
John D. Hancock

Editor
Kingdom Builders Publications

Cover Design
LoMar Designs

Photographers
John D. Hancock
Marie James

The Heart of an Introvert

When one's mouth is
stuck closed and your
heart is yearning to be
heard just let your
fingers echo the
triumphs, defeats,
heart aches, heart
breaks and all of life's

John D.
Hancock

TABLE OF CONTENTS

ACKNOWLEDGMENTS

I would like to thank my family, friends, and co-workers who continuously encouraged me to publish my first book of poems. I wrote most of my poems during my college years so I must also say thanks to Wofford College and my graduating class of 1985.

Special thanks to my dear wife, Constance W. Hancock for her support.
Thanks also goes out to my three wonderful book reviewers, my dear friend Kevin Waites, Betty Gist, Enrique, and Judy Curiel, who graciously retyped all my poems in a suitable format to present to the publisher. You all were instrumental in my journey, and I appreciate it immensely.

The following individuals were so very kind in reading over my work and providing positive feedback.... Heather Phelps, John Sircy, Karen Acosta, Nazharee Cloude and Taleeyah Covington.

I must proclaim that without my dear mother Joe Ann Hancock nothing would have been accomplished. Mom has been my rock my go to person when life's circumstances get tough.
Thank You Mom.

TIME

A Time for laughter

A Time for joy

A Time for You

A Time for Me

A Time for Heartaches

A Time for Pain

A Time to forget

your old love and of

course find something new.

Time to wake up and face

life as it really is.

Time for this

Time for that

Oh! My Father will I have the

time to do them all?

May 6, 1981

A FRIEND

A Friend am I.

One who cares.

One who wishes you the best.

One who is understanding.

One who is thoughtful.

The One who loves you the most

But yet he's only a friend.

December 10, 1981

IS IT?

Is it wrong to be?

To be what I am?

Is it wrong to achieve?

For is my life to be that what those about me want?

No! to be, to be,

I must be what I must be

And do what I must, to be what I am to be.

March 24, 1982

TOUCH

A Touch of love, that's oh so tender.

It makes me feel so good Inside.

Yet, I'm so far, but still so close to you.

Only to relive those moments

of joy we shared.

Oh, in case I haven't told you,

I really do love you.

April 30, 1982

JUST WRITING

Life itself is full of surprises.

Some you meet with a smile,

Others you frowned about and

tried to hide the hurt inside.

Endless nights you dream.

You hope.

You wish for something or someone special.

You search and search.

Where will it all end?

Do you know? Do they know?

Oh, of course, GOD knows,

But why not me?

December 29, 1982

What is LOVE if it can't be expressed without saying a
word?

Often mistaken for lust,

Often stepped on and tossed about.

Often misused and abused.

Sometimes causing pain, always causing warmth to those
who know what it really is.

It's not red. It's not blue,

Not even yellow, but it's love in its purest form that I hold
for you.

Oh, yes, It's true that love is intangible, odorless, colorless
and distasteful to those who know not the secret of love's
power.

But how blessed we are to know love's secret.

November 13, 1983

ENCHANTED

I rose to the top

Yet only to drop.

My every moment was

One of joy, but now

I spend sleepless nights

Yearning for that which

I once had.

Your love seemed so close then,

but now it's gone.

And yes, here I stand broken-hearted

amidst this cloud of doom.

I could wish for more,

But hope lives no more.

Not for me, not for that which I once dreamed, and

lived for so long.

Again, I say I rose only to fall short of that which

I wanted and Loved.

YOU.

December 17, 1983

HOW CAN I?

How can I get to you?

Can I take the express?

or do I have to wait in line?

If a tear or several drops fall

While I wait, will you comfort me, or will you reject me as
always?

Look into my eyes and you will see.

See what, you say?

Well, you will see the pain I

went through just to be

True to you.

Endless nights I tossed and turned.

What am I doing to myself?

Forsaken and Forgotten is my

Heart which lives no more.

December 17, 1983

ILLUSION OR DISILLUSION

There's something on my mind.
Something strange. Something that's hard to
explain. Something I really can't bare
to live with.
I think I know what it is; as a matter of fact,
I know it's you.
I don't know, but there's just something
that won't let me forget you.
I don't know why I keep hanging on.
People talk about you as though you are a toy.
A toy in which they can do with as they please when they
please.
I know some of the things you do and the
people you are with.
No, I'm not checking up on you.
It just so happens that when they talk
about you, I'm there.
I can't stand to hear all the talk.
And yet I know what you do is of your own choosing.
But I can't stand to hear people talk about you,
Every word hurts me more than
You'll ever know.
I may be wrong for feeling this way,
But having you as part of my life
Is all that matters.
And if these thoughts spoken here on this page be invalid
then away shall they go like the wind, and from, there my
heart shall linger where it may.

December 22, 1983

HERE'S TO YOU

To hopes that life's treasures will be yours.

Moment after moment filled with joy and happiness

And if pain and sadness should come,

Think of this rose and remember it represents the love

and understanding I hold for you.

and if words should lose their meaning, then look upon

the brightest star and it will be a symbol of how I will feel

about you, as long as I live.

January 7, 1984

WHAT

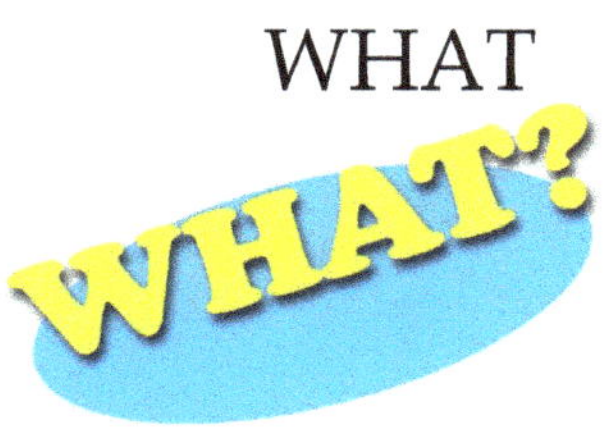

Well, you asked me what I do when I'm alone?

Well, I'll tell you. I just sit and remember the things we

both cherished and loved once.

Remembering the moonlit nights

we strolled down the isles

of paradise hand in hand, heart to heart.

And amidst the joyous thoughts and

memories, comes that burst of sadness

and denial that would befall me, if you

should ever leave.

And knowing what it would do to me

I just blot it out of my mind.

And now remembering that this is all just my imagination,

I tell you I just sit and think of you,

When I 'm alone.

January 29, 1984

YOU

That wondrous figure of beauty and elegance

that's taking the world by storm,

Creating whirlwinds of love

and passion for all to get caught in.

Raining drops of pleasure which words alone will never
define.

You, that wondrous figure of beauty and elegance,

That sparkle in my eye, that smile on my face, that
warmth which flows through my veins,

That dagger that butchers my heart every chance it gets.

Oh, how I treasure and dream of you.

January 29, 1984

POEMS

Knowing that God made

all that which is about me

and recalling that someone

Once said, "Only God can make

A tree and only fools write

Poems", and truly, I must say

that the first is true and if

the succeeding one is true, then

I shall be a fool and write

poetry all the days of my LIFE.

September 1984

LONELY PINE

No water to wet my roots,

No rain to trickle down my leaves,

Nor wind to blow them around and around,

No woodpecker to give me a peck or two,

No snake to crawl down my branch;

Only students to slam books upon me

And mutilate my surface with thoughts

Of love and personal philosophies.

Why must I bare the toil and hardship?

When I can be among the trees of the forest.

WILD FLOWER

Whose Fragrance pleases me more?

Whose petals radiate beauty as far as

The eye can see and beyond?

Whose elegance subdues every heart and

Every mind?

Who reaches the depth of my soul and

Causes it to tingle?

Who stands amidst the heat of summer?

And the blinding snow of winter? It's you, my wild
flower, and for you

I shall be true through all seasons and

For all the countless reasons.

MY PEEP HOLE TO THE WORLD

SUCH A NARROW VIEW

THAT'S NOW SLOWLY CLOSING.

WHEN ALL THE WORLD

REJECTS ME THEN

ALL

SHALL STOP

AND I

SHALL

LINGER

AMIDST

THE DARKNESS

OF DEPTHS

OF

MY MIND.

October 28, 1984

WHAT WOULD YOU DO?

When the news travels like the rushing winds

And all hearts and minds have been stained by its breeze,

What then do you do?

And when the word gets back to you that all is lost,

And your dreams and hopes becomes nothing, but a
puddle of tears.

What then shall happen, my friend?

Should you turn and run until all that is lost, is all behind
you?

or stand and wave goodbye to the future?

Well, my friend, what would you really do?

October 28, 1984

STARSHINE

Beyond the mystic shores of paradise

Shines but one star of radiant beauty.

Tis its beauty and delightful warmth that makes

My heart flutter.

And indeed no man dares to relinquish such

A love light from his sight.

For with that light comes more than

Meets the eye.

An array of passion, a sea of understanding,

A nest of exotic dreams and fantasies to

Make every day worthwhile.

A LIFE ENDED

A life that one cherished so dearly has ended.
And now tears blanket a life which only months ago,
was one of hope and excitement.

Tis these tears accompanied by a host of rushing emotions
and
Thoughts,
Tears of anger,
Tears of sheer hopelessness,
Tears of denial, and, of course, tears of never ending
sadness.

Truly as long as I live, I'll never forget
Such a short lived life which touched my heart so dearly
and surely I'll never stop yearning for that life which has
passed on.

I won't live in the past nor stop seeking out
and obtaining that happiness which lies in the future.
Again, I say that I will not linger in the past, but look to
the future and to my God for the understanding of those
things of which I know not how to interpret or
understand.

December 29, 1984

29

STATE OF MIND

Oh, how funny, you are to lure yourself

Into such a state of thinking,

A state in which you wish all to believe.

A state which is often changing perspectives

And dimensions.

A state which remains out front allowing

Your true state to remain quite anonymous.

Yet regardless, your brilliance and talent

Dazzles even those who think you quite odd and perhaps

Even crazy.

Thus, it is likely you will continue to remain in this state,
but just a reminder, pretend

You may but never forget or lose touch with

The real you.

December 30, 1984

DREAMS

In a place where dreams are mere illusions of

That which is to come

And reality is just the acting out of those

Dreams dreamt by many.

I pose to you this question: When dreams

Become as vague as a misty night, and

The dreams you dream become neither memory nor reality

And reality itself has changed into a maze

Of nightmares, what then must be the distinguishing

Factor, of that which is really real and

That which is a dream?

January 19, 1985

IT HAPPEN IN THE HEAVENS ONE NIGHT

Dancing in the night, Surrounded by flashing

Waves of emotions.

Your heart resting on the Big Dipper and mine

On the Little Dipper.

Both reaching out ever so aggressively to meet

And become one.

And as they reach, the stars tell a tale

Of a truly glorifying waltz which moved even

The distant Planets to quiver.

And surely on this night, the Milky Way proclaimed

The uniting of these two hearts.

BIRTHDAY

On a day that deems it necessary that you
proclaim yourself a year older,
I imagine there are many thoughts rushing
through your mind.

And perhaps many conflicts you wanted to
have resolved in a year's time remain yet
unsolved.

And even though time itself does not stand
still in order for you to enjoy this day to the fullest,
you can still smile because in a year's time, you have
grown to know the Lord, and Savior Jesus Christ for
yourself.

And as you take time to read this card, I would like
to say that also within that years' time, you met
John Hancock.

Whether that's good or bad;
Here's to a very sweet lady.

March 16, 1985

IT ONLY

It only takes a stroll back in time

to reveal the meaning behind days gone by,

In which I sat awake staring beyond today,

Looking to yesterday, and now awaiting tomorrow.

For so precious, and purely divine was each moment,

For you were my special gift from Heaven and to

Heaven I turn my eyes in thanks, for prayers of

Yesterday answered today.

And I know that my tomorrows will be full of thoughts of

you, never lingering too far and always listening.

And perhaps always fearful of that which is to come.

But yet you see it only takes a stroll back in time to

See why it's so meaningful.

June 11, 1985

LEAVES

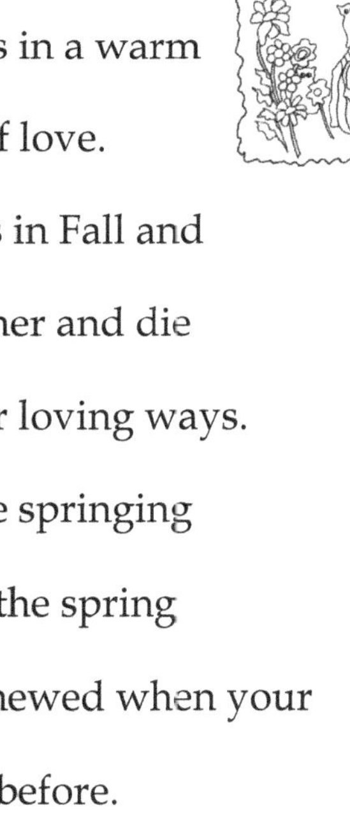

Like the leaves of a tree soaking

In the sunshine,

So here my heart soaks in a warm

and comforting pool of love.

And as with the leaves in Fall and

Winter, I began to wither and die

when you change your loving ways.

Tis I know that like the springing

forth of new leaves in the spring

My heart is forever renewed when your

loving ways return as before.

and then once again I'm like the leaves

of a tree, just soaking in your pool

of warm and comforting love.

June 24, 1985

DISSIPATING TIES

It's nice to look back and

Think of all things

We shared and loved so.

And, yes, it was a joy knowing

And being with you.

But nothing we shared and loved will

Cause me to give up my hopes for

Tomorrow.

ONE MOMENT

It takes only a moment to rationalize this situation.
And yet as I look back, it took so long to let my heart
Go out to you.
Then loving you and experiencing love was such a joyous
and
Pounding urge that took me to resorts of pleasures
I never knew before.
And each passing day found me filled so much with a
burning desire,
To proclaim to even the distant stars
This sparkling glare in my eyes
and the awesome pounding of my heart.
But then something happened and my heart barely
Flutters, and my eyes stare ever so distantly
beyond the walls of yesterday,
not wanting to look ahead,
Knowing you won't be there.
And now remembering like never before how great
The feeling was to be in love,
And as I remember, the changes that I'm now going
through
Seem to never stop causing pain.
And now it should take only a moment to rationalize and
Understand why the walls exist.

July 1985

AND IF

And if love should choose not
To come again, then so shall
It be.
And if stupidity is an unknown
Factor to the heart, then so shall
It be.
And if you choose another, then so
It is what you desire. And so shall
It be.
And if my heart lingers on loving
You whether you choose to love
It or not, then so shall
It be.
And if it is my heart that loves
You, and not this old frame of
Mine, then so shall
It be.
And in so much as my heart
Is the only part of me that
Is an ever living being, then
My love for you shall never die and so shall
It be.
And truly if you love my body
As my body, and not because
It is the temple of my heart; then so shall It be.
And so shall my body remain and my heart
Shall linger on in love with you.

ODE TO A BLACK WOMEN

Oh! What pain you have suffered,

What joy you have brung,

What wisdom have you shared.

And Oh! For a fleeting moment with you,

I, the Black Man, have ever watched and waited

As a Black Man I stand for many things:

LOVE, HATE, STRENGTH, WEAKNESS, JEALOUSY
AND COURAGE.

In courage, I shall face all those wrong things

I have inflicted upon you.

Like a trapped animal, I have lashed out against you and
the world.

I have caused you great pain in many ways.

I in my hour of default I have failed you.

Yet, in love, I have found the strength to overcome

My jealousy and my weakness.

And in love, I have found understanding.

And in love I have grown to hate that which causes the
moments

With you to be ever so fleeting.

And in so doing, I the Black Man, have found in myself

A new sense of being, a new foundation on which to
build, a new spirit of being

A TRUE BLACK MAN

IN LOVE WITH

THE BLACK WOMAN YOU ARE.

YOU'RE NOT ALONE

You're not alone in your sorrows or grief;

There are people who share your hurt and

On that you must place belief.

You'll never stand alone for he who knows all

Knows your heart, mind and soul.

So when the things you do turn your peers away,

Remember that you're not alone but that your

Disposition tends to make them stray.

For he who knows all things sometimes allows

You to stand alone and examine the situations;

"Am I the cause or am I just being thrown like

A stone?"

And in your loneliest hour, look upon yourself and

Ask yourself, "Have I forsaken myself?" if the

Answer is yes, others have realized it too, and

Admittance is the first step in helping yourself.

However, when the world about you seems to grow

Ever so dark, he who knows all will light your

Path so you can see your way back to the light.

So, if ever you think you're all alone, remember, he who
knows all will forever stand by you and if you turn
slightly, you'll find that I'm always there, too.

"NO MAN IS AN ISLAND NO MAN STANDS ALONE."

IF EVER

If ever our paths should meet, I only ask of this,

Please greet me with a smile to let me know and show

That you care.

For I have often thought of this moment when I would

Reach out and communicate with you again.

When last we talked, I was overwhelmed by the inner

rage

And hurt I have brung upon you.

I have suffered much because of this pain I have caused

You, and in my own way still yet grieve.

And if ever our paths should cross, I will only greet you

With the biggest of smiles to let you know that I find

No pride in causing hurt or pain, but indeed the joy

You brought to me still yet flows.

And I suppose that I will often wish for, IF EVER OUR

PATHS SHOULD MEET.

I'VE WALKED THIS WAY

I've walked this way before, over and over again in

My mind, I've walked this same path.

I've always wondered what it would be like while I

Was walking that way in my mind.

But now that I'm actually feeling the feelings and

Thinking the thoughts, it all seems so different

Than when it was all in my mind.

For the feelings that I'm now feeling seem to continuously

Cause pain.

But yet when I look at you, the pain goes away; and things that

Could be and should have been, reappear again in my mind.

And again I'm no longer walking that path of sorrow and hurt.

But I'm loving you with all my might and more.

And yet, now it seems all right because you, too, are returning

That love I have shown you.

Yet, it seems so unreal because I've never thought that

Such a love ever could be possible other than in my mind.

And still yet, I must say that I've walked this way before, but

Only over and over again in my mind.

LEAVING

Leaving seems to be the proper thing to do.

But, yet in leaving, it means I have not given you all

The love you need.

And in this, I can't seem to get it out of my mind that

I have not fulfilled your needs.

You know I wish not to leave, even though leaving is

The proper thing to do.

I hurt so, inside until this numbness has overcome even

My deepest emotions.

And when crying seems to be the answer to relieving this

Anguish, no tears will form or fall.

But, even in the absence of tears, it isn't difficult to see

All the hurt.

And yet leaving is the proper thing to do when it comes to

You and me.

JUST SAYING

In all that I have done, in all that I have seen, and In

All that I have had done to me,

I have concluded this one fact.

It is better to be in the company of my enemies than in the

Midst of my friends.

In the presence of my enemies, I remain ever so alert,

while I become rather relaxed and somewhat complacent

when I'm

With my friends.

And time has shown that my friends are the ones that

have used me

Time and time again.

And in truth and all honesty, it is my enemy who is my

friend,

And my friend who is my enemy.

BUBBLING OVER

Bubbling over with laughter and joy, I come yet
Again to your door step.
Bubbling over with joy and laughter, I come again
Seeking that warm pool of love that I once soaked in
for so long.
And bubbling over with joy and laughter, I have again
come up short.
For bubbling over with laughter and joy, I come yet
again to your door step, only to find that, that which
was once yours and mine,
Is now yours and his.
And as the bubbling laughter and joy turns into hurt
and tears, I find myself yet again leaving the same door
step, that I once could call my own.

ASHLEY

Upon first glance, mine eyes were upon you, and knowingly no

words could ever express what went over me,

Never having felt this way before I turned my eyes unto the

heavens, pouring my heart and

soul out.

Many nights had passed, knowing you were not near, and I

wept until my eyes were dry and

my heart torn.

And then something happen and undoubtedly I know it was a

miracle.

You were no longer far and yes my tears were now those of

extreme joy that perhaps no one

will ever know.

For even then things were slow, but the miracle kept near, and

things were soon fine.

And now as mine eyes behold such a sight I value each passing

day much more now that you are healthy and well.

For with every step you made my heart cried out and my soul

searched the heavens thanking that miracle maker who made it all

possible for you and me to be together.

And together forever shall our hearts remain, gleaming with

undying love and joy.

SUMMER BREEZE

Summer breezes of days of love gone by,

Summer breezes of days gone by,

Summer breezes of days to come,

Summer breezes, summer breezes, still yet on my mind,

Summer breezes and summer pleases me to be with you.

BLISS

Oh, bliss of heaven, truly divine

Fixed upon the wings of a dove, covered with thy precious blood.

Not moved by the doctrines of men nor demons.

Would that I could see thee this night.

Oh, bliss of heaven, capture me, rapture me and take me to heaven dear Lord.

DAY

Yes, it's another day in love with the Lord,

And love gets sweeter and sweeter as the days go by,

OH! For the love of God I shall endure.

Let my tears reflect your love.

Let my tears reflect your grace.

Let my tears reflect your mercy.

Let my tears reflect the joy you have given me.

Yes it's another day and your love has not stagger nor

has it swayed.

NIGHT

Oh, fragrance of night, of rain and honeysuckle; in which I do delight in your odor so bright.

Oh, the beauty of this night.

Oh, how I wish that my tears would fall as the rain of this night.

Not in pain, but in pleasure and longing for a love so dear.

I am overwhelmed by the beauty of it all, and a still persistent yearning to go home.

Oh, Jesus thou has surely visited me this night in the gentleness of your might.

Oh, how I love thee and honor thee this very night.

I PERISH! I PERISH!

From this present world into eternal light.

For I perish in the flesh, and awaken in heavenly light.

Born of the Spirit, washed in His blood; and lead by His Spirit.

Soon to be quicken by the Spirit, to be given rest in eternal light.

AUTHOR

Take flight with this author as he goes and has gone through the perils of love, emotions, and hurt.

In the midst of a dying world, lost without morals, on the edge of despair and destruction.

But yet rejoice for this author has found life in death.

EXALTATION

What man seeks to exalt himself?

Although many exalt themselves and await the exaltations of others the question still remains.

What man seeks to exalt himself?

To be exalted of man is but a curse, but the exaltation of the Lord

is far greater and just.

To be exalted of the Lord is to know suffering and endure it, to know humility and desire it, to know the role of a servant and seek it.

To be exalted of the Lord is to know brokenness and require that it exist.

Seek the exaltation which comes from Jesus Christ that you may know of His sufferings and the burden that caused Him to endure the rugged cross.

RAIN

I can hear Heaven in the rain drops, as they tell of Jesus,
who died for you and me.

And as they drop the flow of His blood crosses my mind
and smites my heart.

Oh! What love and mercy they speak of.

Oh! What suffering;

Oh! What pain;

Oh! But for the love of mankind and a burden that ceased
not, until Calvary.

Oh! For Calvary was where His blood flowed and
dropped like rain,

Oh! Thankful am I for the drops of rain that take me back
to Calvary.

TRUTH OR ERROR

There is always truth before error, before one can err,

there must first be truth to err from.

Before Satan, there was God.

Before Adam, there was Jesus Christ.

Before wrong there was right.

Before illicit sexual practice,

there was purity in the confines of marriage.

Before Abraham was I Am and likewise before Baal,

Buddha, and all the other gods of men was **I AM**.

HE WON'T

Jesus can't, won't, and doesn't

have to die again for humanity.

But humanity has to die for Him again and again

and moment after moment.

QUESTION

Can a man have faith

enough to bring about healing through his faith?

and yet not have enough faith to surrender

his life totally to Jesus,

and in turn die and go to hell?

TRUTHS

Proclaim to the hills, mountains and

heavens above that the opinions of

men neither change nor make void

the truths of God,

For it has been stated:

*HEAVEN AND EARTH SHALL PASS AWAY, BUT
MY WORDS SHALL NOT PASS AWAY.*

Matthew 24:35

AN EGG

An egg when it is hatched
No man when viewing with the
naked eye can see what grows inside.
Yet when the warmth of the
mother or incubator is applied
constantly and continuously over
time,
a baby chicklet is born.
Yet if one would have of one's
own accord broken the shell
before time, no chicklet would
have come forward.
And so it seems with the seed of the
word when it is received by some,
there is no outward sign
of that which is growing inside.
Yet when the warmth of the
word,
and the heat of the word of God,
is constantly and continuously.
Over time a baby convert is
born.
Yet if one would have of one's
own accord broken the shell before
time no convert would have come forward.
Yet in God's time babies are born.

SONG OF PRAISE

In the arms of Jesus I shall not stray.

In the arms of Jesus I shall not fall.

In the arms of Jesus I shall always be.

So hold me Lord, hold me Lord

and cleanse me through & through

(REPEAT)

Oh, watch me Lord,

Oh watch me Lord.

Both day and night.

(REPEAT)

For in the arms of Jesus I shall not stray.

EMOTIONS

Waves of nothingness that seem to go and come.

Sometimes often and sometimes not.

Waves of nothingness, whether of pain, of joy, of

warmth, or of love, they

all last but a moment.

Nothingness, nothingness that's what it is when love is

all gone

and even worst if hope is gone with it.

Waves of nothingness a truly never ending saga.

"BEHOLD"

Proverbs 31:10

For you have gathered the youth of thy years to stand
in a day of uncertainty.
But rest in peace for thou Husband is known and
stands at the Gates.
For thou Husband is a man without equal, a man of
passion and a man of strength.
Oh, virtuous woman in whom shall thou heart delight
and what is the desire of thou heart?
"Strength and honor are her clothing; and she shall
rejoice in time to come." Proverbs 31:25
Oh, virtuous woman knowest thou the heartbeat of
thou Husband?
Shall he rise and call thee bless and call thee or has thou
left thou dearest Husband standing at the gates of thou
heart?
Oh, virtuous woman in a time of uncertainty leave not
thou Man of passion and strength standing at the gates of
thou Heart.

"BEHOLD A VIRTUOUS WOMAN"

MY HEART ECHOES

My heart echoes cherished thoughts of YOU
Many days gone by thinking of the gentleness of your
touch,
the comfort of your smile and hearing you say I love
you.
You're my rock, you're my hero who's always been
there for me through the joys of life, and the rocky roads
we've traveled.

My heart echoes confidence in knowing that the love
we share will never die.
Never die you say? Yes, Never Die!
My heart echoes the peace that surpasses all
understanding,
The LORD above shall render unto YOU, or I should
either one of us have to say good bye.
Saying good bye isn't easy, if we leave each other and
enter the comforting arms of the LORD, no doubt in my
mind the wonders and the awesomeness of YOU will
never fade.
The bliss of winter, spring, summer and fall all spring
forward through the gentleness of your touch.
My heart echoes cherished thoughts of YOU.

ABOUT THE AUTHOR

John David Hancock, Born 1962, in Fort Lawn, SC to

Marion and Joe Ann Hancock. the author was at one time a big time introvert. A 1981 graduate of Lewisville High School in Richburg, SC John went on to earn his bachelor's degree in psychology from Wofford College in 1985. While at Wofford he joined the Army ROTC program where he was commissioned as a second lieutenant in May of 1985 serving until 1994 when he was honorably discharged from the US Army as a Captain. John went on to become an assistant manager with Bojangles in Columbia, SC in March of 1986 where he stayed until he was hired by the Richland County Sheriff's Department in March of 1987. John served in law enforcement for over 32 years, serving the citizens of Richland County until May of 1993 and in October 1993 he joined the SCDHEC police force where he served until 1996 at which time the police force was transferred to the South Carolina Department of Public Safety's Bureau of Protective Services Division. He served with SCDPS/BPS until July 1, 2020, when he retired as Chief of Police.

John is an advent outdoorsman who loves to fish, hunt, go hiking, and sit by the fire pit to mediate and pray and to go strolling along the beaches regardless of where they are. He is a servant at heart helping those in need while working with his Blythewood Rotary Club and volunteering to assist the SCLEAP (South Carolina Law Enforcement Assistance Program).